IN THE
NATIONAL INTEREST

General Sir John Monash once exhorted a graduating class to 'equip yourself for life, not solely for your own benefit but for the benefit of the whole community'. At the university established in his name, we repeat this statement to our own graduating classes, to acknowledge how important it is that common or public good flows from education.

Universities spread and build on the knowledge they acquire through scholarship in many ways, well beyond the transmission of this learning through education. It is a necessary part of a university's role to debate its findings, not only with other researchers and scholars, but also with the broader community in which it resides.

Publishing for the benefit of society is an important part of a university's commitment to free intellectual inquiry. A university provides civil space for such inquiry by its scholars, as well as for investigations by public intellectuals and expert practitioners.

This series, In the National Interest, embodies Monash University's mission to extend knowledge and encourage informed debate about matters of great significance to Australia's future.

Professor Margaret Gardner AC
President and Vice-Chancellor,
Monash University

INALA COOPER

MARRUL: ABORIGINAL IDENTITY & THE FIGHT FOR RIGHTS

MONASH
UNIVERSITY
PUBLISHING

Monash University Publishing
Matheson Library Annexe
40 Exhibition Walk
Monash University
Clayton, Victoria 3800, Australia
https://publishing.monash.edu

Monash University Publishing brings to the world publications which advance the best traditions of humane and enlightened thought.

ISBN: 9781922633248 (paperback)
ISBN: 9781922633262 (ebook)

Series: In the National Interest
Editor: Louise Adler
Project manager & copyeditor: Paul Smitz
Designer: Peter Long
Typesetter: Cannon Typesetting
Proofreader: Gillian Armitage
Printed in Australia by Ligare Book Printers

A catalogue record for this book is available from the National Library of Australia.

The paper this book is printed on is in accordance with the standards of the Forest Stewardship Council®. The FSC® promotes environmentally responsible, socially beneficial and economically viable management of the world's forests.

My writing was done on the unceded lands of the Boonwurrung/Bunurong and Wurundjeri peoples of the Kulin nation. I pay my deepest respect to them, their Elders and ancestors, and extend that respect to all Aboriginal/Torres Strait Islander people who read this book.

MARRUL: ABORIGINAL IDENTITY & THE FIGHT FOR RIGHTS

This story starts with my paternal grandparents, two people I never met but whose influence on me and my family is profoundly felt.

First, it's important for me to acknowledge that my Elders had to fight a different fight from my own. Many of the themes are the same: sovereignty, voice, treaty, truth-telling, access, justice, recognition, rights. But as time changes, so too do attitudes and society in general. My story illustrates some of these changes, including how the strength of Aboriginal/Torres Strait Islander people endures, how we share and teach, and how we exude excellence. No longer are Aboriginal/Torres Strait Islander people and our histories kept invisible. Now we are taking up space—more space, the space that was always ours on this land. Our stories are on TV, we are seen in parliament, we are doctors, engineers, lawyers, community leaders. Our cultures, our traditional and contemporary ways of knowing, doing and being, are continuously being amplified, on our terms.

My grandmother was Patricia Mary Djiagween. If she had not passed before I was born, she would have heard me call her Nanna. I've learned about who she was, and about parts of her life, from my Uncle Patrick, Aunty Fay, and assorted other family members who remember her with a sad fondness and tell stories of her staunchness. Storytelling is precious, and I'll be forever grateful for all the little tidbits I've heard and the long yarns I've had with family out at 'the block' in Broome, and during humid evenings in Darwin. They take my mind and my imagination back to the late 1930s, when Nanna Patricia was at risk of breaching the Western Australian *Native Administration Act* of 1936 because of her relationship with Abu Kassim bin Marah, a Malaysian man who was under threat of deportation for the same reason. Abu Kassim was the father of my aunties Fay and Georgina and my late Uncle Gerald, who lived for just two hours.

I've been told about the young couple's disputes with authority, and their confusion around how Abu Kassim's child maintenance payments would be accessed by Patricia. They wanted to marry but knew it would probably not be permitted. In Uncle Patrick's words, 'They had to beg for their rights [but] they were not the begging kind.' Neither am I.

In May 1941, the inevitable occurred. Nanna Patricia and Aunty Fay were arrested under section 12 of the Act and sent to Beagle Bay Mission, about 100 kilometres north of Broome. There, six months later, my Aunty Georgina was born. A little while later, in early 1943, Patricia requested permission to leave the mission and return to Broome—the request was denied. At this stage she was well known to the authorities, and her reputation was not in good shape. Inspector O'Neill of the Broome police wrote to the Native Affairs Department after my enraged Nanna (allegedly) punched the priest at the mission, Father Francis, to the ground. He described her as 'one of the ringleaders ... a bad example and influence to the others. She deliberately flouts the rules and regulations of the Colony'.[1] An unsurprising statement from someone enforcing racist legislation, and a familiar sentiment of power and control that continues in the relationships between Australian governments and Aboriginal/Torres Strait Islander people today. O'Neill recommended Patricia's removal to Moola Bulla, a government-run station near Wyndham. Control of her movements and her associations was part and parcel of being Aboriginal.

Aunty Fay related her time at Beagle Bay to me some years ago. She said that after Nanna punched Father Francis, the two of them plus Aunty Georgina were put in the Beagle Bay lock-up. Nanna and her two girls were then transported to Derby and on to Broome to await the cartage truck to Moola Bulla. On the way they stopped at Christmas Creek, and it was there that Patricia met my grandfather, John Murray 'Snowy' Dodson. The man who, if he had not passed before I was born, would have heard me call him Pop.

Snowy's story is a bit of a mystery. There are few to no records of where he was from or how he made his way to Christmas Creek. The family recall that he was good with his hands and found employment easily as a mechanic, driving trucks and working on cattle stations. But questions about his background remain unanswered. Was he a stowaway who arrived in Darwin on a plane? Some family members say he was an Aboriginal man from Tasmania. Others say he was likely Irish. Whatever the case, he was enamoured with my Nanna, and at Christmas Creek, Pop Snowy took her and my two young aunties with him as he absconded with the cartage truck towards Lamboo Station. They were found two weeks later, and the authorities sent Nanna and her girls to Moola Bulla. Their stay there was short, as Pop Snowy went up there with his semitrailer and lifted them again, and they managed to stay out of the hands of the authorities for the next two months. I can only imagine that being on the run, sadly, may have felt normal to them.

The family was found at Brooking Springs Station. The law at the time was clear: a (person deemed to be a) White man and a Black woman and her two kids couldn't be allowed to be together. So Pop paid an enormous price for loving my Nanna, in the form of eighteen months' hard labour, a requirement of the Act, at Fremantle Prison. The court did not formally punish Nanna, only in that she was sent back to Moola Bulla with Aunty Fay and Aunty Georgina, 'longing for her love' (in the words of Uncle Pat).

I'll pause here for a moment to let all this sink in. This is not just part of my family history, this is part of Australian history and Aboriginal/Torres Strait Islander history. And it is recent history, clear in the minds of my aunties and other Elders today. The mistreatment and disregard for Aboriginal rights and humanity is as heartbreaking as it is shameful. The next part of the story resonates with me deeply because I never had to ask permission from anyone to marry my husband. This is the privilege that I have been afforded due to the struggles faced by my ancestors.

Pop Snowy was forced to apply for permission to marry Nanna Patricia, in April 1945. The application was rejected, and an order went out for all letters exchanged by my grandparents to be intercepted. The level of supervision and coercion applied to Aboriginal families in Western Australia was draconian, racially motivated and actioned with vigorous force, in ways that non-Aboriginal families have rarely experienced. This continues in many other forms today.

The control imposed on my family was relentless. My great-grandmother Elizabeth Fagan— Granny Liz—had no option but to write to the authorities in November 1945 to ask permission for Patricia and the girls to return to Broome; in her ageing years, she wanted her daughter and granddaughters around her. The request was denied, with the explanation that Patricia had 'been involved with Asiatics' and that her only option was to find domestic employment on a station in the Kimberley. Further evidence that the Act, the enforcers of the Act, and White control at the time were racist to the core.

My grandparents were eventually reunited when Pop Snowy got an early release from jail in late 1945. He arrived in Moola Bulla to find Nanna Patricia pregnant, the result of a relationship with a stock-man from New South Wales named Cecil Rose—the product of that union would be my Uncle Cecil Adrian. The authorities swooped on this situation and determined that Aunty Fay and Aunty Georgina were to be placed in the Broome orphanage. Granny Liz came to collect her grandchildren, desperate to save her family, and eventually managed to keep Uncle Cecil out of the orphanage by committing to caring for him at home. This devastating period was par for the course according to the Act, but it would change my Elders' lives irreparably. We must not

forget at this point that the removal of Aboriginal/
Torres Strait Islander children from their families
is not something relegated to the past. It continues today, with just as much pain, confusion,
bureaucracy and racism.[2]

Nanna Patricia and Cecil Rose had intended
to marry, but Rose made off from Moola Bulla,
refusing to sign a maintenance order for his boy,
saying he was now uncertain of the paternity.
Nanna then went to Wyndham and had her young
son with her when she reconnected with Pop
Snowy, and their love blossomed once again. They
were now, according to Aboriginal lore, married.
For their marriage to be recognised by the state of
Western Australia, however, government approval
still needed to be granted—until then, they were
each at risk of imprisonment. This permission was
finally given, and Nanna and Pop were married
at Halls Creek on 8 September 1947. There is one
photo of them on their wedding day, copies of
which are dearly held by the whole family. From a
young age, I gazed lovingly at these Elders I'd never
known, yet who had a distinct familiarity. I didn't
realise just how similar some of my features are to
Nanna's until one of my friends once remarked that

I was the 'dead spit' of her. I imagine Nanna would have liked that and seen herself in me. Nanna Patricia and Pop Snowy's marriage was sadly not without conditions, however. According to the Act, they were now required to leave Western Australia.

Nanna and Pop proceeded to have Aunty Fay and Aunty Georgina released from the Broome orphanage, with Nanna also awaiting the birth of her next child. By this time, Abu Kassim bin Marah had returned from serving in World War II, and he joined forces with Pop Snowy to play illegal dominoes in Sheba Lane in Broome to help his daughters' mother secure the girls' custody. They won, of course, and as they handed their winnings over to the nuns of the convent that served as the orphanage, Pop Snowy rejected the offer of government blankets, exclaiming: 'Shove them up your arse.'[3] From the late 1790s to the early 1800s, government blankets were purposely infected with smallpox in the hope of killing off Aboriginal children,[4] so in the interests of protecting his family, Pop's judgement was to be cautious of any authority figure bearing gifts.

On 29 January 1948, my Uncle Patrick was born in Broome. To my great-grandfather Paddy

Djiagween, he would be known as Minyirr-bul—
'Broome Boy'. Departing the well-trodden trail of
forced poverty, repeated imprisonment, removal
of kids, separation from homelands and blatant
racism, the family travelled to Katherine in the
Northern Territory, looking for a fresh start and,
deservingly, fairer treatment. For now, Nanna and
Pop left Aunty Fay in the care of family in Derby,
and Granny Liz continued to raise Uncle Cecil,
while the couple ventured north-east with Aunty
Georgina and the newborn, Uncle Pat. Pop Snowy
gathered what he could to make a small house for
the family behind the old meatworks, and although
nobody turned their backs, I'm told they were never
fully welcomed into the town. There grew a percep-
tion that the family was 'on the edge of survival and
chaos'.[5] Aunty Fay joined the family in Katherine
after the birth of my Uncle John Murray (Jacko)
in Darwin in 1949, and she helped deliver the
next two babies, who would complete the family:
my dad, Michael (Mick) in 1950, and my Aunty
Patricia (Patsy/Tricia) in 1952.

Uncle Cecil was taken to and from Katherine,
remaining in the care of Granny Liz, whose movements were still being tracked by the authorities.

A protector from the Native Affairs Branch then removed her from a pearler camp in Darwin and sent her back to Broome. It was cited in her file that it was not considered desirable that she remain in Darwin. How dare this legislation control her movements because of who she was, her heritage, her appearance. How offensive, hurtful and damaging to our family, and indeed to the place we now call Australia, that legislation such as this can seek to keep Aboriginal/Torres Strait Islander people and their families in a place of constant diminishment.

There is much more to this part of my family's story, to the experiences of my Elders, but it is clear that the lives my grandparents lived, in which 'there was goodness, there was badness',[6] were controlled at every turn. Their rights were consistently denied because of their Aboriginality, circumstances and love for one another. But they wouldn't stop fighting for justice, and neither will I.

∼

The history of this country, this continent, is often glossed over by shiny documents like

Reconciliation Action Plans (RAPs). They can be useful, they can also be useless, but the question of whether Australia has achieved Reconciliation, or is on the way to achieving it, requires more than aspiration to answer. I don't believe Reconciliation is a destination, that there is necessarily an end point. Rather, it's an ongoing process, something that each community and generation must decide upon. To be reconciled with our past—with White Australia's past (and present)—it is not enough to ask if we are achieving Reconciliation. We must ask if we are achieving justice. And if we are to have justice, Reconciliation is not enough. There must also be a sharing of wealth and power, there must be truth-telling, and there must be a recognition of Aboriginal/Torres Strait Islander sovereignty.

We have never ceded our sovereignty, which makes the British claim of sovereignty over our lands, waters and skies valid only by their law, not ours. Our sovereignty means that Aboriginal/Torres Strait Islander people were, are and will continue to be self-governing. It means we have an innate connection to country that will never cease to be. The places we come from and are connected to tie us to our songlines, ancestors, cultures and lores.

They provide our contexts, our understanding of the world and of our place in it.

I was a child when I first heard the word reconciliation, in a different context, at Karella. It is a place I can never forget, the place where I first felt at home. Although when I think about home, I feel pulled to two very distinct places. As a Yawuru woman, when I think of my home of Rubibi/Broome in Western Australia, which is where my dad's family come from, I get images of the sparkling blue ocean, warm sun, red dirt and humid winds. I imagine the ancestors I never met: Nanna Patricia, Granny Liz and Pop Snowy, retrieving my aunties from the orphanage. I remember holidays of long days spent at Cable Beach and balmy evenings at the block. Men build the fire and prepare the meat; women make the salad and the rice. We sit outside in an area that used to be a thoroughfare, a meeting place. The breeze is gentle and comforting.

The place where I grew up has a very different landscape, but my connection to it is just as strong. Pyipkil (or Ummut) is the original name for the place now known as Port Fairy, in Victoria's south-west. Pyipkil/Port Fairy has icy kelp-laden oceans, volcanic rock, and in winter, fierce, howling winds.

I imagine the Gunditjmara warriors in that wind: staunch, protective, reminding us of the ancient ways, the ancestors, the fight.

I mostly learned about the land from my maternal grandfather, Desmond Patrick Crowe (Des). Born on the kitchen table in windy Codrington in 1922, he was of Irish Catholic stock and was a farmer his whole life. My grandmother, Joan Cecelia (nee Uebergang)—yes, we all called them by their first names—was a farmer too. They each had their roles and grew healthy, valuable wool, lamb and beef for over fifty years on their patch of Codrington: Karella, meaning southern wind.[7] My mother Alecia, (late) brother Minnira and I lived at Karella with my grandparents for a time in the early 1980s, and they were some of my happiest days. After the three of us moved into our own place in Port Fairy, weekly visits to the farm were maintained. Karella was positioned between neighbouring farms and along the Princes Highway, where you could look across to Woodlawn where Des was born: my great-grandparents' farm. Beyond that were sand dunes and the vast Southern Ocean. It was a magical place to grow up in, a place where I ran with cousins through the fruit trees, down to the dairy and over to the creek; where weddings, Easter and Christmas get-togethers, all kinds of celebrations were had. It was the place where I learned that the land is not only (or just) a resource, but a relative—and that justice comes in many forms.

There is so much to touch and see on a farm, so much to discover about the place itself, and about yourself. The space is wide, the air is fresh, there is so much country. And it was Des who taught me about it. Like how to smell rain coming, when to tie things down before a big wind, never to open a gate without then closing it, how to chop thistles, when to irrigate, where to mark out a fence, how to show respect for the creek, how binder twine can fix almost anything. It was inherent in his (and everyone else's) practice on the farm that if you looked after the land, it would continue to produce, to care for and nurture us. Des also taught me about the animals through his respect for them. It might seem strange that a farmer should show respect for animals being bred to produce meat, but he genuinely cared for them. As a child, I could see we were not better than them, but at the same time, in the world of the farm, we had a right to them: their eggs, their milk, their meat. Some complexities make us stop and contemplate status, rights and balance, but sometimes life itself is so much louder and present, and the complexities don't demand interrogation.

A kid's rite of passage on the farm was learning to ride the horse, or 'the pony' as Des called him. There's something about getting up close and personal with a large animal that can either make you fearless or scare you so much you can't move. But once you'd trotted Trigger around the yard a couple of times, you earned a certain rank among the cousins, similar to that of ride-on-mower rights. This status didn't mean you were exempt from hard work or helping, though. We still encouraged everyone to have a go, especially if they were littler than ourselves. And we still had to shovel the manure out of the yard (Joan needed it for the garden). There was never any waste on the farm. I learned about sustainability before I'd heard the word, following Joan to the veggie garden and back, helping her shell peas and de-silk the corn.

Some nights we could hear the distress of an animal in the distance and Des would have to go down the paddock with a torch to help a cow birth her calf. I remember seeing a calf being born once, in the yard. I was fascinated at how and why Des had his arm inside the cow, all the way up to his shoulder! The slippery animal ultimately emerged to my squeals of delighted horror. A bit like the time Des took me across the paddocks in the tractor, and when he pulled up, he pointed to a tree and said: 'Look at that tree and don't stop looking at it 'til I tell you to.' Obedient me stared straight ahead for a good five minutes, when I heard a gunshot. I didn't move. Eventually, Des climbed back up on the tractor, turned it round, and as I watched, amazed, he hooked the beast he'd just killed on the back and we returned to the shed. I sat up on a ledge and looked on as he carefully butchered it. Soon enough, Des told me to run up to the house to get Joan, and she and I returned with freezer bags and a texta—no need to go to town for meat. For some, I'm sure it could have been a completely traumatising experience, but I just accepted it as the natural order of things and tried my best to be a good granddaughter of the farm.

We had just the right balance of freedom and rules for kids. Joan ran a tight ship and high expectations were put on all of us, particularly regarding our manners and behaviour, no matter where we were. Respect was instilled in us from day one and enforced via a range of powers including God, Santa and the wooden spoon. Don't go down to the creek by yourself. Don't climb up the silo ladder. Up at the table for tea at six. Up early every Sunday for church—no exceptions.

Joan did all the girls' hair. We had to grow it long—there was no cutting it until you were at least twelve years old. Bodily autonomy? No. You'd stand to attention at the bench with Joan, who would be armed with a brush, a bowl of water and a biro. The biro was to ensure you had a straight, even part. All us girls got a blue line down the back of our necks for church. Joan would dip the brush in the water and whack it on your head. Did you know you have little hairs on your ears? You do, and Joan was an expert at brushing them back into your tightly woven plaits (ouch!).

Routine was important on the farm. After church there would be a hot roast lunch, then we'd be sent outside to play. The news coincided with dinner (although I have to say that, as country folk, we all called it 'tea'), and it was at the farm where I started learning about politics. During the day, the wireless would alert us to the news with the ABC's flourish of majestic horns on the hour. We were told to shush as Des and Joan, and every other grown-up in the room, listened in. Tea was always a quiet event because of the news, and even more quiet was demanded when *The Gillies Report* came on TV, raucous and hilarious. We all watched on as Max Gillies gave the viewers a class-act performance every week, satirising our then prime minister, perfectly capturing Bob Hawke's 'utter self-belief'.[8] Seeing how a comic actor could make fun of the person holding the highest office in the land showed me how politics can be easily communicated and translated to the masses. It was a format we could all access and understand. It was even more intriguing to see footage of Bob Hawke and Max Gillies together—talk about breaking the fourth wall!—Gillies always in character in those moments when he was face to face with his subject. I was fascinated as a young performer about how the meeting of a real person and their caricature worked. Gillies showed me how to sustain a character and maintain the illusion, preserving the fantasy that emerges from such a commitment to performance. Hawke showed me a style of leadership I will always be striving to attain.

~

Pyipkil/Port Fairy is part of Eastern Maar country, and it's windy, guaranteed, particularly in winter. Cold, strong, howling winds coming up from Antarctica, chilling the spine, invading earholes and making your eyes water. Even in the discomfort of the wind, however, I never feel that it's trying to harm me. Yes, there are hot, glorious, cloudless, sunny days too. They give me just as much affection.

In Port Fairy, you'll feel the wind everywhere: at the East Beach, leaning against your car bonnet at The Passage, and on the hill where St Patrick's church sits on the Princes Highway. The church is a large building, built in the Gothic Revival style of the mid-1800s from local basalt courtesy of the volcano at Yatt Mirng/Tower Hill. Named after the patron saint of Ireland, the church is evidence of the strong Irish Catholic community that settled in the town they first named Belfast. It was completed in 1859, and baptisms, funerals, first communions and weddings continue to be held there. Grandfathers dab their eyes, bridesmaids dash to control the bride's veil, and children scamper in the car park all riled up before the service—all because of that wind. Every time we left the church, the south-west wind hit us as we walked out the arched doorway, blasting across brow and breast wet from blessing yourself with holy water, reminding you that you'd done the right thing for another Sunday. At least a quarter of an hour would be spent out front catching up with people. From an early age, I realised that church was not just about God and praying—it was a social outing.

St Patrick's Primary School in William Street is just a short walk from the church. It was here, when I was nine years old and in Grade 4, that I was told to 'make my reconciliation'. We were living in Port Fairy at that time, but we frequently made the twenty-minute drive west to Karella, keeping very close to Des and Joan. I had found out from my grandparents that reconciliation was another word for confession. I knew what confession was. I'd heard them talk about it before. I'd seen them go into the confessional booth at St Joseph's in Yambuk to tell the priest their sins. You were supposed to keep your sins secret, though; you weren't allowed to tell anyone what was spoken in the confessional booth. I wondered if the wind, which crept into the church from under the doors and down from the bell tower, would capture people's sins and take them up to Heaven to be set free.

A lot of time was spent preparing us Grade 4s for our reconciliation. We were told that it meant telling the priest all your sins, and if you were truly sorry, you would be forgiven. Our teacher gave us examples of sins, to help our young minds dig down into our naughtiness to work out how to articulate it. Perhaps you had used a bad word. Had a fight in the playground or talked back to your mother. Lied about something. The teacher told us it was OK. If you were really, truly sorry and said your prayers, you'd go to Heaven. The admission of your wrong-doings, of your guilt, meant you would be saved.

The church was a safe and familiar place to me. The wooden pews were smooth to touch. The smell, even the cold, was comforting. Nervous as I was about making my first confession, I kept telling myself that as long as I was honest, everything would be alright. The priest wasn't allowed to tell anyone about your sins, so no-one would know what they really were. Afterwards, I was praised by my mother, other family members, the teacher and the 'church ladies'. Now that I knew how to admit my sins, I felt a bit more grown-up and responsible.

On I went through primary school, 'doing reconciliation' every couple of months or so when it was scheduled at St Patrick's. The meaning was very clear to me, and I remember 'saving' sins when I was naughty, thinking, 'I'll have something to say at reconciliation now.' Sometimes I lied and made sins up because I couldn't think of any. 'I was mean to my brother' was a good default admission.

The meaning of reconciliation changed for me around the age of twelve. I was now a high-schooler, catching the bus from Port Fairy every day to St Ann's—soon to become Emmanuel College—in Warrnambool. The wind was a bit different over there. It was still cold, strong and guaranteed, but it smelled different. On a good day, you'd get the aroma of coffee coming from the Nestlé factory. On a bad day, you'd get choking, pungent wafts of dead animals from the abattoir. As reliable as the wind was, it was not as safe to me as the Port Fairy wind.

St Ann's had been founded by the Sisters of Mercy, who came to Australia in 1846 all the way from Dublin. I once spent forty-eight hours in that city, visiting colleagues at Trinity College, and even in so short a time, I felt a connection—including on the night spent enjoying a traditional Irish band belting out 'Star of the County Down' at the Temple Bar pub, while I stood shoulder to shoulder with a merry crowd of strangers, sipping my Guinness. How I long to return and explore Dublin properly, and visit the places my Irish ancestors came from: County Monaghan (via Granny Liz's father, Joe Fagan) and County Clare (Des's ancestors, the Crowes).

Emmanuel College originated in 1991 on the amalgamation of St Ann's and Christian Brothers College. I had been delighted to spend Year 7 in a glorious whirl of girls-only classes, excursions, performances and sports days. When Year 8 and the amalgamation came, I remember confessing to a priest that I didn't like the boys—my romanticised view of pretty white bobby socks and sweet-smelling classrooms with flowers and lip gloss through to Year 12 was in jeopardy. By Year 9, though, I'd gotten over it, made friends with the boys, and was thoroughly enjoying school.

The early 1990s saw me discovering a new interpretation of reconciliation and seeking to learn more about how Aboriginal/Torres Strait Islander people could get justice due to past wrongs against them. This was the time when Paul Keating made his famous Redfern speech, St Kilda footballer Nicky Winmar showed the Collingwood cheer squad his skin, and we had the International Year of Indigenous People (1993). Something was changing, and it was Mum who did a lot of the explaining. The TV and the radio were the places where I most saw and heard Dad at that time. Native title legislation was being drafted and Dad had been invited to contribute, along with other Aboriginal leaders including Marcia Langton, Lowitja O'Donoghue and Noel Pearson. He was ensconced in the world of the United Nations (UN), and in his new role as the first Aboriginal and Torres Strait Islander social justice commissioner. He also worked on two royal commissions: Aboriginal Deaths in Custody (1987–91), and the Separation of Aboriginal and Torres Strait Islander Children from Their Families (1995–97). I learned to feel proud when my teachers at school said, 'I heard your dad on the radio this morning!' I knew the work he was doing was important, and he helped me grow my strong identity, even from afar.

I remember, in 1992, watching Keating's Redfern speech on TV and talking with Mum about why people were emotional about it, why everyone was talking about it, why it meant something to Aboriginal/Torres Strait Islander people. Around this time, the Aboriginal and Torres Strait Islander Commission (ATSIC) and the Reconciliation Council (now Reconciliation Australia) were established. I was fourteen, which, now that I'm in my forties, I realise was a most impressionable age. Seeing replays of Keating's speech over and over on the news, what rang in my ears were the admissions he made: 'We took the traditional lands ... brought the diseases ... committed the murders ... took the children from their mothers.'[9] I felt amazed that the prime minister was *actually saying* these things.

Keating also said, 'We failed to ask—how would I feel if this were done to me?' Having grown up a Catholic, this statement stayed with me. One of the first things I had learned both at Karella and St Patrick's was 'Do unto others as you would have them do unto you'. The prime minister was admitting sins and wrongdoings, revealing guilt. Keating told Australia that 'there is nothing to fear or to lose in the recognition of historical truth'. I knew that reconciliation meant telling the truth, and I wondered if the wind on the block at Redfern would carry the country's sins away. But it was too unfamiliar a place for me to know.

I was starting to see Reconciliation as a public thing, with a capital 'R', no longer confined to church confessionals. The media and my family were showing me that Reconciliation was something which the whole country needed, regardless of Catholicism, Christianity, any religion. I discovered the role that White Australia had to play in delivering justice to Aboriginal/Torres Strait Islander people. Admissions of truth were needed, and I had already learned that apologies should be given freely, without the expectation of a response, let alone forgiveness. God forgave, but that was very different—this was about sovereignty, survival, resistance, justice and rights.

However, the characterisation of that fight for justice, and the protection of the rights of Aboriginal/Torres Strait Islander people, as requiring an act of reconciliation, which has its origins in Christianity, should give us pause to critique the process and the ideology on which it is based—as many Indigenous scholars and activists have done.

Makarrata is the Yolngu Matha term for a peace-making process: the coming together after a struggle. This somewhat aligns with how the word reconciliation is used in religious contexts, but makarrata has a deeper, more complex meaning. It is a philosophy belonging to the Yolngu through which peace can be maintained. The word and the gesture translate easily to White Australia. However, there has been a mix-up over how Reconciliation apparently requires a considerable amount of acquiescence (politely eating cupcakes at Reconciliation Week morning tea) and generosity (being expected to give advice and do other work for free) from Aboriginal/Torres Strait Islander people. It is not *we* who need to do the reconciling. It is those who, to use the Christian vernacular, have *sinned*, and who continue to sin. The settlers, the colonisers, the invaders, the British, the White Australians: it is they who must listen to us, learn from us, and work with us, not only to reconcile but to ensure justice and truth-telling. This work cannot be a one-way endeavour. To achieve Reconciliation and justice, truth-telling must be combined with the sharing of wealth and power and an overhaul of the systems that White Australia has created to keep Indigenous people and communities from flourishing—even, in many ways, from existing.

The reimagination and complete transformation of these systems is a two-way street. It is not enough to make admissions without anything then being changed. This takes courageous leadership and strong collaboration with Aboriginal/Torres Strait Islander people and communities, within which our self-determined solutions sit.

So at fourteen, I was trying to wrap my head around everything to do with what it meant to be Aboriginal. This was the first time Aboriginal people had been invited to contribute to creating laws. The *Native Title Act*, while important in protecting how we govern our land, is imperfect legislation. One of its flaws is that it allows the government to extinguish native title through compulsory acquisition by the Crown, without a cent of compensation payable. The burden of proof— that communities/claimants have an unbroken, uninterrupted connection to their land—is also problematic when that proof is examined and decided upon by the government and courts of the very colony that displaced us; too many miscarriages of justice have occurred because of this. But those who worked alongside Keating to get native title up knew that they had laboured too hard to now sit back and do nothing. Native title is not the same as land rights. Land rights are our birthright. Our relationship with the land is one of connection, not ownership in the Western sense. We are bound to protect the land—it is our provider, our mother. Many Aboriginal/Torres Strait Islander people before me have written eloquently on this, including Professor Gary Foley, Professor Larissa Behrendt, Professor Uncle Tom Calma and more.

I saw more of my Uncle Pat on the TV than in person at this time, too. Uncle Pat was once a Catholic priest, and he'd officiated over the marriage of my mum and dad in St Patrick's in 1976. The photos of his ordination in Broome the year before include the only images I've seen of my Granny Liz; my dad's resemblance to her is striking. Mum explained to me that Uncle Pat couldn't do the work he wanted to within the church and that was why he was working on the Reconciliation 'stuff'. I learned so much about my identity via Uncle Pat's example and guidance. Here was a man who could apply his experience as a priest, with more than one interpretation of what reconciliation could be—a deeply spiritual man who was (and still is) tirelessly working for justice. I began to comprehend through his work, and Dad's, the layers of complexity that Aboriginal/Torres Strait Islander people embody. I came to understand the conflicts that exist between Catholicism and our inherent Yawuru spirituality. Aboriginal/Torres Strait Islander people are not one homogenous group: our cultures, lores, customs, complexities and range of life experiences guide each of us in our pursuits.

After he left the priesthood in the early 1980s, Uncle Pat worked in a range of social justice roles, including as a director of the Central Land Council, the Kimberley Land Council, and Nyamba Buru Yawuru Ltd, and as a commissioner (alongside Dad) on the Royal Commission into Aboriginal Deaths in Custody. Notably, Uncle Pat worked hard to establish what is now known as Reconciliation Australia. When my husband and I married in the very same church as Mum and Dad, we called on Uncle Pat to share his wisdom and guidance by giving the homily. He has a way of translating things for all manner of people with grace, humility and a gentle authority that stirs you and will have you thinking about being in his presence long after.

~

The only prime minister I can remember before Keating is Bob Hawke. He was the first prime minister I heard talk about treaty, land rights and native title. I was ten in 1988, when Australia was celebrating its bicentenary—200 years of British invasion/settlement. In anticipation of this event, the theme chosen for the 1987 National Aboriginal Islander Day Observance Committee (NAIDOC) Week was 'White Australia Has a Black History', a slogan which illustrated Australia's well-established reluctance to acknowledge Aboriginal/Torres Strait Islander sovereignty, and the truth of the colonial project on our land. A new commitment was aired by Hawke at this time, after his visit to the festival at Barunga in the Northern Territory—that a treaty would be made to acknowledge the unique rights of all Aboriginal/Torres Strait Islander people, as a way for the country to move forward with respect for our sovereignty. The year 1988 was filled with Australian nationalism, parties with people draped in the Australian flag, the World Expo in Brisbane, a re-creation of the arrival of the eleven ships at Botany Bay, and rightful protests by the continent's First People, demanding we be seen, heard, acknowledged, and receive justice. What emerged around the treaty and land rights conversations was a division between those who would not pause and seek to understand—those who held racist views about it—and Aboriginal/Torres Strait Islander people and communities, and our allies, who were fighting hard, seeking the protection of our rights, including treaties.

With Hawke having made public and very vocal commitments to treaty and land rights legislation, there must have been some belief, some hope back then, that finally Aboriginal/Torres Strait Islander people would see some justice. I was just a child and could only watch on in silence at the farm, taking it all in as the grown-ups discussed what difference it might make. This was not the first time there had been promises, beliefs or hopes of treaties and justice. The Yirrkala bark petitions were the first documents asserting native title prepared by Aboriginal people—the Yolngu of Arnhem Land—and presented to parliament, in 1963, to the Menzies government, in an act of sovereignty intended to create legislative change and constitutional reform. In 1972, the Larrakia people brought their petitions to then prime minister William McMahon, who also rejected them.

Then the Barunga Statement was presented to Hawke in 1988. Discussions of treaties and land rights were met by some fierce opposition within Hawke's own party, including from then WA premier Brian Bourke, who supported the mining companies in their public scare campaigns. In the words of Labor MP Linda Burney, it was racist, venomous, ugly and feral. The Opposition said that, as soon as they could take office, they would tear up any treaty Hawke dared to make with Aboriginal people.

It's 2022 at the time of writing, and we are still waiting for any treaty to be signed, in any jurisdiction of Australia.

Hawke should have stood his ground. I don't understand why a leader such as he didn't do so, why he wouldn't keep his promise. How could he have stood on Yolngu country after receiving the Barunga Statement and declared a treaty would be made, and not follow through? Is it all easier said than done? It's not within my ambitions to enter politics, but as a citizen, a taxpayer and a sovereign Yawuru woman, the least I should expect is that a prime minister keeps their word. I remember seeing Hawke on the TV, weeping during a press conference, dismayed that his government would not achieve treaty. He expressed his disappointment as he asked his 'Aboriginal friends' to understand that 'more could not have been done'. Dad was at that press conference, and when the camera panned across to him, I saw a sovereign man who had perhaps lost all hope in that moment, a man looking utterly bereft, an image now etched in my mind. Years later, the miniseries *Hawke: The Larrikin and the Leader* showed former Australian Council of Trade Unions secretary Bill Kelty remarking that Hawke 'failed not because his heart wasn't in it, he failed because his heart wasn't in it enough … if you believe in things and don't do them, there's sadness'. Profoundly true, on all sides.

Towards the end of 1991, the song 'Treaty' by Yothu Yindi was everywhere, coinciding with what would be the end of the Hawke government. Thirty years later, we still have no treaties, but some Australian jurisdictions are progressing with the process, including Victoria, where a Treaty Advancement Commission was set up in 2018, which in turn, the following year, established the First Peoples' Assembly of Victoria. Early in 2022, the assembly held the Treaty Day Out on Yorta Yorta country in Shepparton, at which Yothu Yindi performed an electrifying version of their renowned song. Everyone sang along, everyone knew all the words, everyone danced as we once again demanded 'treaty now'. Thirty years we've been singing this song and I don't think we can say we've progressed the way we thought we would have back in 1988. It's not for lack of trying, though. Aboriginal/Torres Strait Islander people have never stopped putting in the work. The song reminds us of the many barriers, including 'all those talking politicians'.

~

After high school, I was busting to get to Melbourne and into university and working life. Church confessions happened further and further apart, and Reconciliation remained a public thing. ATSIC was dissolved, Dad became a co-chair at Reconciliation Australia and an academic at the University of New South Wales, then at the Australian National University, and he also took on the inaugural Aboriginal and Torres Strait Islander social justice commissioner position. The media were calling Uncle Pat 'the Father of Reconciliation', and

I started to hear people talk about Reconciliation as 'something that makes White people feel good about themselves'. My view of what Reconciliation was or could be, and how it applied to me, was evolving. Reconciliation with a priest is private, while Reconciliation between Aboriginal/Torres Strait Islander people and other Australians (as well as they with themselves) is public, and I was working out how I felt as I tried to embrace it.

In 2010 I started working at Monash University. By that stage I had spent three years in the Victorian Public Service and had been looking forward to the new environment. Although Port Fairy had grown me accustomed to wind, it wasn't until I came close to the Robert Menzies Building that I knew what the Melbourne suburb of Clayton was capable of. It was as if the Menzies, the Union, the Law school, the Gallery and the Rotunda had conspired with the wind to test the students. I wondered whether, if you could brave the wind to get inside and learn, would you be 'saved'? Had the wind been this bad when the Menzies Building was the 'skyscraper' which stood out there in the middle of nowhere, or did that not happen until the 'Ming Wing' received companions? I didn't know. I just huddled into my coat and tried to avoid my papers being scattered everywhere as the unforgiving wind whipped me around campus.

At Monash, the word Reconciliation was around me every day. A bright light was being shone upon it as the first Reconciliation Action Plan came to life. The focus of the RAPs is on relationships, respect and opportunities, a template prescribed by Reconciliation Australia. At the time I worked to embrace these words as an important part of what Reconciliation meant, but I'm not sure if I was able to separate the word reconciliation from words like confession, truth and forgiveness. In church, you achieve reconciliation once the priest absolves you of your sins, and you promise to act to remedy the wrongs you have done. I do not know what our country will be like if or when we achieve Reconciliation—much less truth, justice, reparations, 'land back', or an acknowledgement that it is not we who need to do the reconciling. Also, if Reconciliation does not have an end point, how will we know when we have achieved it?

I know the answer is not in the wind but rather inside us—although as with the wind, if we face the truth head-on, it may cause our eyes to water, rile us up, mess our hair, and knock things over. But sometimes that's what needs to be done to get up the hill to St Patrick's, out to the block at Redfern, or into the Menzies Building. The wind has memories in it and stories to tell us. We should listen to it not to get all the answers but to find our own way to truth and justice—each generation's form of Reconciliation.

We can't talk about Reconciliation without talking about racism, because why do we need Reconciliation in the first place? The racist nature of the invasion and settlement of our country, and the ongoing discrimination against Aboriginal/ Torres Strait Islander people, is why. There is also a need for settler Australians to come to terms with its history, its biases, its prejudices, as well as its willingness to engage with and learn about Aboriginal/Torres Strait Islander people and cultures. The truth of both our past and present must be brought to the surface and reckoned with. How else can this nation move forward with a healthy and whole identity based on respect? It's important to also recognise that Reconciliation presumes the existence of peace between two equal parties. Professor Gregory Phillips, a Waanyi and Jaru man, says that while Keating was well intentioned, he got it wrong—Reconciliation can't be the way to frame our history (or our present), not least because it reinforces White power and supremacy.[10] Phillips is right, but I continue to refer to Reconciliation here to suggest to White Australia that it does need to reconcile itself with the fact that wrongs have been committed on this land in the name of the Crown.

The hesitation and fear surrounding the surfacing of truths stem from how this disrupts the status quo—the status, privileges and freedoms experienced by non-Indigenous, mainly White people in this country, which are protected at all costs. This is evident through countless examples, including the consistent failure by the Commonwealth to meet Closing the Gap targets, substandard levels of health care, the blowing up of sacred sites by mining companies, and the persistent incarceration of our people that results in shameful and devastating numbers of Aboriginal/ Torres Strait Islander people dying in custody. We rise—*yimijalan* in Yawuru language—then we are pulled back down. It cannot be said enough that the systems created by Australia are not broken. Rather, they have been intentionally designed to diminish us, humiliate us, imprison us, get rid of us. We are well overdue for an overhaul. Australia can start by putting our own matters back into our own hands. Relinquish the arduous and unnecessary power wielded over us by diverting funding and control to Aboriginal/Torres Strait Islander community organisations. We know how to look after our mob.

When racism occurs, it should be called out and action must be taken to remedy it, every single time, including by changing mindsets, policies, procedures and entire systems. These are steps towards justice. In schools and workplaces, for example, people need to be supported to identify racism and learn how to call it out. Look no further than the remark grown adults have made to me, 'I didn't learn about this at school', as if the only learning we ever do is at school. First, if you're a grown adult, you've likely got a device that fits in the palm of your hand and with which you can access almost any piece of information ever generated, so start doing the work yourself. Second, the huge absence of Aboriginal/Torres Strait Islander histories, peoples and cultures in school curricula has occurred by design. I had teachers repeatedly tell me that Aboriginal culture was dying out, which was devastating for a child to hear. It negated my existence, translating as: 'You must be like a White person to survive.' Whether comments such as these, and the attitudes they reflect, are expressed overtly or covertly, they will inform the culture of an environment. The falsehoods many of us are taught can evolve into persistent, toxic truths.

Many schools in Australia are getting better at including Indigenous knowledge and perspectives in the curriculum and in day-to-day activities. The schools I went to never flew the Aboriginal or Torres Strait Islander flags or made acknowledgements of country. These gestures are important ways in which to begin teaching children about showing respect for Aboriginal/Torres Strait Islander people, and for Indigenous kids to feel some pride when they are at school. We are finally moving away from an education system which in many ways was planned to present only one image of Indigenous people on this continent, one deficit narrative, in order to maintain White supremacy in our society.

Aboriginal/Torres Strait Islander organisations are doing amazing work to increase our visibility and embed our cultural perspectives into curriculum. For example, Culture Is Life, led by staunch Wotjobaluk/Dja Dja Wurrung woman

Belinda Duarte, is collaborating with production houses and education experts to create strength-based materials for schools. One such partnership, with the ABC, focuses on First Nation connections with nature and the landscape, merging Indigenous science and cultural knowledge to create an engaging experience for young people.

This is but one example of how Aboriginal/Torres Strait Islander excellence benefits everyone and provides a means of reshaping our education system. For too long we were viewed as curiosities, possessions, mere savages, and early colonial attitudes sadly still pervade contemporary policies and systems. Connecting Aboriginal/Torres Strait Islander knowledge, excellence and hard work with people who lead mainstream systems and are ready to make change—that is the key. Then, not only our schools but our workplaces, universities, football games, real estate agencies, taxis, hospitals and so on can become safer and more just places for us to be in.

At this point I want to be clear on a very visual and inherent part of my identity, which is the colour of my skin. I acknowledge the privilege I have by being 'light-skinned' or 'White-passing'.

Genetics is a fascinating thing, and I know that I am assessed and judged (rightly or wrongly) by the various features I have inherited from both my parents. I also know that my appearance has nothing to do with whether I am Aboriginal. During the years I spent working in hospitality and retail as a student, customers would constantly inquire about my ethnicity, particularly when I was wearing a name badge. These were the 'But where are you really from?' and 'What are you, though?' questions, to which I would reply, 'What do you think I am?' Predictably, the answers always went like this: 'Italian?' 'Greek?' 'Macedonian?' 'Maltese?' 'Spanish?' 'Turkish?' (Insert any other European ethnicity here.) When I replied 'Aboriginal', once again the responses were predictable. These were the 'Oh, but you don't look Aboriginal!' and 'Oh, that's OK though!' comments, the most distasteful of which was: 'But you're so articulate!'

The one that has always stayed with me I heard one summer evening in Port Fairy when I was playing out in the street with the neighbourhood kids, with our parents standing nearby. I overhead someone saying that an Aboriginal family was moving into the street and they didn't want them there.

Mum stepped in and said, 'My kids are Aboriginal, and we've been here for years, they've been playing with your kids for years.' Their reply? 'Yours are different.' Thousands of other Aboriginal/Torres Strait Islander people have experienced interactions like these. They demonstrate to us the way in which our governments, education systems and media portray us, the low bar that is set for our success, the lack of humanity and dignity we are afforded as people, and the imposition of White notions of identity upon us. They are also just plain racist. It is not a compliment to tell us we're different to 'others', or to remark on how articulate we are. Our ancestors were flogged for speaking in language, so yes, of course we are (your version of) 'articulate' (in English).

It is part of my experience that I am treated differently than other Aboriginal/Torres Strait Islander people who have darker skin, including people in my own family. I acknowledge that my experience of the world is different because I am not targeted because of my skin colour. The discrimination I face is not the same as that faced by those who are followed around shops, refused a seat on a bus, spat at, locked up for minor infringements, or—devastatingly—shot dead by police. Being Black and appearing Black are two different things in this country, and the systems created by the colony have a ruthless way of maintaining this. I can't help but think about how my son will inevitably be treated differently to his cousins by the system, due to his fair appearance. The targeting and policing of Aboriginal/Torres Strait Islander people are shameful and unjust, even more so when an overwhelming number of victims look only the way the media and the state want people to view us.

~

Change takes effort and commitment, and that commitment must be real and evident among non-Indigenous leaders and decision-makers. You can't address racism simply by having a RAP and holding a morning tea to say you're sorry. As Bidjara/Birri Gubba Juru woman Aunty Jackie Huggins has said, it's about more than just making friends. Reconciliation and justice require truth-telling, reparations, the sharing of wealth and power, and compensation. Thinking back to the sacrament of reconciliation in church, if you have a proactive priest who is invested in their congregation, who gives practical advice and guidance, there's a greater chance of good resolutions and outcomes between people. A lazy priest who does not care for their congregation's wellbeing will just instruct you to say ten Hail Marys and tell you to come back next week. Effort and commitment in all our environments are crucial if we are to make this world a better place now and for future generations.

The sharing of wealth and power is a concept that is strikingly absent among Australia's authorities and institutions, and it remains something that requires deep interrogation and change. If institutions are serious about Reconciliation—I still want to hear more of them talk about justice—and aligning with campaigns such as Racism: It Stops with Me, then they need to be proactive in reviewing their governance, leadership and ways of working. Employment initiatives, for example, must do more than provide entry-level roles for Aboriginal/ Torres Strait Islander people. Look at who is in the boardroom, who makes up the executive, and who occupies other leadership positions, because the lived experiences of those individuals, combined with the history and culture of the organisation, define how things operate. It is not complicated. It does not require a complex framework or strategy. It starts with respect and humility. Respect for the unceded land you operate on, and the traditional owners' protocols, customs and lore. Respect for our knowledge and excellence we so generously and graciously share. And having the humility to both see and admit that Aboriginal/Torres Strait Islander people display this knowledge and excellence, and ways of knowing, doing and being, which both differ from those of non-Indigenous people and hold extraordinary value.

The practice of appointing people only on merit needs to be done away with, to a certain extent. When people talk about merit as it relates to Aboriginal/Torres Strait Islander people being qualified for or well suited to a job, then the fairness, equality or objectivity that we are being measured against is one that has been constructed by, and is intended to apply to, White people. Thinking back to the comment made one evening in Port Fairy, that my brother and I were 'different' from other Aboriginal kids, this bias indicates that some people think darker-skinned kids are *less than*, are a problem, don't fit in. Bias, both conscious and unconscious, plays a huge role in the application of merit to individuals, and it is a means of maintaining a safe place from which White people can continue to operate the systems in the way they were designed to operate, which is usually (surprise, surprise) by White privileged men, for White privileged men. This reflects the 'more of me' mentality, where leaders and decision-makers surround themselves with people who think like them, look like them, went to the same private school as them—are the same as them.

This is not to say that all White people are inherently racist. But nor does a disruption of who holds the power mean that White people lose anything—rather, everyone gains more. Applying White-constructed merit without any other consideration when it comes to Aboriginal/Torres Strait Islander access, employment and promotion, is flawed because we do not share an even playing field with our White counterparts. We can have the same qualifications and experience that our competitors for roles do, or even more of them, but White versions of merit are too easily used to evaluate how someone will 'fit', instead of broadening the discussion of what Aboriginal/Torres Strait

Islander people can bring to the table. We are also making our own tables, but that doesn't mean we don't belong at the existing ones. Leaders and decision-makers who are non-Indigenous should be equipped to manage their own biases and create safe, diverse environments.

Diversity and inclusion can also be done away with—again, to an extent. They have become buzzwords for organisations that seek to address, or that want to appear to be addressing, the fact that they are dominated by privileged White men. I agree that diversity is important, but what is more important is defining what we mean by diversity, and why we use the word inclusion, and talking about them in a strengths-based way rather than in terms of deficit. Applying a diversity policy does not mean having to make sacrifices to lose talented people. And inclusion reinforces the power imbalance, similar to when kids are being picked for teams at school: will you be chosen to be included or not? Will you represent the 'right' kind of diversity to fit in? Aboriginal/Torres Strait Islander people do not need organisations to try and work out how to 'include' us. We need respect—we demand it. Furthermore, corporatising our skills and contributions by placing an emphasis on 'capacity building', instead of dismantling barriers to Aboriginal/Torres Strait Islander success, or doing the work to create safe spaces where everyone belongs, places the responsibility back on us. We already possess enormous capacity, and if the existing merit lens was removed, more people would see that.

Multiple times in my working life I've experienced how these barriers work, and I share this with the acknowledgement that these encounters can be experienced differently by Aboriginal/Torres Strait Islander people with darker skin than me. When our excellence is on display, when we are meeting our key performance indicators, when we are bringing solutions to problems, the question of elevation or promotion can be quickly shut down. The progression through our workplaces that we deserve can be stifled through comments like 'We just don't think you're ready yet', 'We need to wait until after the review', and the miserly 'Be careful what you wish for'. I have had all of these comments handed to me when I know I'm ready (they know I'm ready too), when I know that the review will recommend more Aboriginal/Torres

Strait Islander people in leadership positions (they know that too), and when I know exactly what I'm wishing for (pay me what I'm worth). What comments like this are really saying is, 'I don't want to lose my power to a Black person.'

Keeping us down is what the systems we interact with were intended to do. Only respect, humility, commitment and effort will change them. The late Professor Uncle Colin Bourke was a strong and gentle Gamilaroi man who devoted his entire career to Indigenous success in education. In his words (from him to me): 'All we need to do is appoint Aboriginal people and support them to succeed. Then we will achieve good outcomes for everyone.'

~

There's a freedom to working at a university that nourishes your curiosity, your ideas, and your way of interacting with the world. Universities are places in which to test thoughts and seek answers, and it is in this environment that I thrive. At the time of writing, I've been working at the University of Melbourne for almost five years. It is a place that challenges me every day due to its history as a big, rich, White, sandstone institution. The fact that I have found comfort here is because I've interacted with such institutions my whole life—and because of the right that Aboriginal/Torres Strait Islander people have to be here despite the racism that exists. I also thrived as a university student. Dad was the first in our family to graduate from university (Mum was pregnant with me at his graduation in 1978) and it was the path I was expected to follow. At the end of Year 12, all I wanted to do was turn my passion into my profession. I had no clue how I was going to do that, but in 1996, Deakin University Rusden helped me begin to work it out.

Performing has always been part of my life and my identity. As a child, I loved making up dances and plays in the rumpus room at the farm. Listening to music, I would choreograph complex routines in my head and perform them for the mirror in my bedroom (OK, I *still* do that!). I took every available dance class, participated in rock eisteddfods, speech and drama eisteddfods, debating, anything that allowed me to express myself—anything with an audience. My cultural identity at the time was very different and very separate from who I was as a performer. At school and university, my arts education was filled with Shakespeare, Sylvia Plath, Henrik Ibsen, the Stanislavski method, Martha Graham, Ted Shawn and Ruth St Denis, Isadora Duncan. I loved it, I immersed myself in it.

Our teachers reminded us that we had to 'know our history' if we were going to succeed as professional actors and dancers. The history they were referring to was particular: English, European, American, White. My birthright, to learn and grow in Yawuru language, expression, culture and traditions, had been stifled by colonisation. As a young Yawuru person in country Victoria, trying to make my way in the world, I was thousands of kilometres from my traditional country. At the time I just wanted to get to Melbourne so I could continue acting and dancing—all day, every day, if they would let me.

I was so eager to learn and to express my creativity that I followed every lead that I could see. But without the internet, with only two TV channels in my tiny country town, and coming from an all-White, all-female country dance school, it was not until 1996, in my first year of university, that I first heard about Bangarra. One of my fellow students remarked, 'You're Aboriginal? Why don't you go to Sydney and join Bangarra?!' I think they were eager to maintain a White classroom and White theatre. Too bad for them. I didn't know what Bangarra was, or who they were, and I felt a little fearful, and embarrassed that I'd not heard of them. But more significantly, as adventurous as I was, my first thought was, 'I'm not going to Sydney. I don't belong up there.' After a bit of investigation of this contemporary dance company, I told myself: 'I can't be the kind of Aboriginal people they are. I can't enter their space as *this kind* of Aboriginal person. I've not been handed a torch.' I had yet to be given any authority from my Elders as a holder of knowledge with a role through which to express and share my culture, or a responsibility to nurture and evolve my culture. I thought I would have no credibility in Bangarra's space. I thought I was not Black enough.

I remember hearing about auditions in Sydney for Bangarra around that time, as well as for the National Aboriginal Islander Skills Development Association (NAISDA). Of course, I didn't go. I don't think I even mentioned it to Mum. What right did I have to be in that space? Or, turning it around, did I have every right? The 'not Black enough' mindset is just one example of how colonisation damages us. I wonder now how my cultural identity, as well as my creativity and skill as a dancer, might have changed had I felt stronger in my Blackness back then, or had I the chance to expand the creative circles I was in. I can imagine what it would have been like to have met people like Rhoda Roberts, Deborah Mailman, and the Page brothers—Stephen, David, and Russell—who founded Bangarra Dance Theatre. Particularly Russell, who was one of the most powerful, mesmerising, daring and beautiful dancers this country has ever seen.

The separation of what I wanted to pursue in my theatre/performance life and who I was in my identity and culture, that didn't bother me as a teenager, but in my twenties it started to change. It was exciting and daunting to learn more about Bangarra and NAISDA, about Black performers who were steadfast, sovereign, fierce, skilled, creative and proud. I hadn't spent much time in Sydney at all. I knew nothing of its vibrancy and history when it came to Black performing arts. Why didn't my university teach me about this? I finally saw Bangarra for the first time in Sydney in 1998, and it was as humbling as it was thrilling.

I had never been exposed to dance in this way before. It opened my eyes, my heart and my spirit. I was witnessing the beauty of traditional culture and movement through a celebration by urban Black people. I was in the third and final year of my degree and contemporary dance was one of my majors. I was dancing thirty hours a week, at my peak physically and mentally as a performer. And watching the Bangarra dancers on stage, I was 100 per cent confident that my technique matched theirs. But I was not confident I could match their cultural expression. It was and remains deep, connected, connecting. It intimidated me. It was only as time went on that I began to realise I *was* Black enough.

Fast-forward to 2012. When Wiradjuri woman Anita Heiss asked 'Am I Black enough for you?' in her bestselling book of the same name, I felt a great affirmation, which had been slowly building since my uni days, that I need only be myself and not worry about being the type of Aboriginal person others want or expect me to be—or that I imagine they expect me to be. It's not that I hadn't felt strong in my identity before then. It was that my world to that point had largely revolved around me making my way through mainstream systems. They were the systems that were familiar to me, and I knew how to navigate them: school, church, the doctor's office, the surf club, dance class, interactions with authority. My lighter skin afforded me a privilege that many other Aboriginal people, even in my own family, were denied. Also, the majority of Aboriginal people around me were my family and people who worked with Dad and Uncle Pat, and they helped me flourish.

During school, I knew a few Gunditjmara kids from Warrnambool and Framlingham who happened to be around the same age as me, and sometimes we'd see each other at interschool socials and parties. I was not close to them, not well connected to their families, or to the broader Framlingham Aboriginal community. I knew very little of their cultures and identities and the ways in which these might be both similar and distinct from my own as a young Yawuru woman. On reflection, I'm sad that I held back from making those connections. I don't blame myself, but it shows the way our minds can be so colonised as to make us think we don't belong in our own community, among our own mob.

Politics can clash with the arts, and in particular it can clash with cultural ceremony and expression through art. But of course, politics is not always White on Black—there are politics within communities themselves. In *Firestarter: The Story of Bangarra*, Artistic Director Stephen Page talks about meeting with First Nation leaders and community members—the 'biggest mob', he says—who were calling for an Aboriginal/Torres Strait Islander boycott of the Sydney 2000 Olympic Games. Stephen recalls a meeting in which he said, 'We can't not have a presence inside that stadium ... because that girl's got to run that race.' He was talking about Cathy Freeman, who was 'all of us' in the moment she lit that cauldron, and who carried the hopes and dreams of the entire country as she went on to win gold in the 400 metres.

Stephen's reflections on this, his approach to the role he had as artistic director of the First Nation component of the Sydney Olympics opening ceremony, are indicative of the complexities of being sovereign First Nation people in this country. We do not and cannot exist in isolation as Aboriginal/ Torres Strait Islander people. We have responsibilities towards each other which cannot be ignored, because they have been inherited, and because they continue to evolve. We have deep connections to each other which go back over 65 000 years. Stephen's leadership, the effort he made to ensure that Cathy was not in that stadium on her own, that the whole world would see who we were as Aboriginal/Torres Strait Islander people, was profound.

I felt privileged to meet Stephen at the National NAIDOC Awards in 2016, when he was honoured with a Lifetime Achievement Award. I introduced myself and we yarned for a few minutes. 'You a dancer, hey?' he asked. I hesitated: 'I used to be.' 'Nah sis,' he replied. 'You were born a dancer, you'll always be one.' Even though my life and career have moved away from the stage, I recall this exchange from time to time. It reminds me that I have something innate, skills and creativity that are a combination of things I had to work extremely hard at to learn, and things I was born with. So yes, it's been a while, but I am (still) a dancer.

～

It remains a constant source of frustration: the alarm and upset expressed by White people when they see a news story which illustrates the racism and elimination of rights experienced by Aboriginal/Torres Strait Islander people. I'm not saying White people shouldn't be alarmed and upset, but when they express this urgently to us, as if we are only just discovering the injustices at the same time as them, it adds to the pressure placed upon us to do something about it, rather than the focus being on the perpetrators.

These are moments of truth-telling which make White Australia extremely uncomfortable because the news story is in fact a mirror. ABC TV's *Four Corners* has revealed a range of injustices imposed on Aboriginal/Torres Strait Islander people. The 2015 program 'Remote Hope' highlighted the living conditions in some remote communities. Then prime minister Tony Abbott described the poverty and scarce job opportunities as a 'lifestyle choice' and declared he would not subsidise them. Such an ignorant comment perfectly reflected his life experiences and attitudes towards who deserves to be supported and who does not. The premier of Western Australia at the time, Colin Barnett, agreed and threatened to shut down 273 remote Aboriginal communities, describing them as not sustainable and suggesting that the children there were being abused.

In early 2022, another *Four Corners* story, 'Heart Failure', told of young people in the community of Doomadgee in Queensland who were needlessly dying from rheumatic heart disease, a preventable condition. The story highlighted the racism embedded in the Queensland health system, describing how sick people—mostly children—were repeatedly given paracetamol through a grate at the local hospital's emergency triage area and sent home instead of being examined. These were children who needed lifesaving surgery, the details of which were supposed to be recorded in their patient history records. In the report, Gudanji-Arrernte woman Pat Turner, CEO of the National Aboriginal Community Controlled Health Organisation, said what we've all been thinking and saying for years: the government continues to fail our people and we are tired of it. If this had involved a White kid in middle-class Sydney, there would have been an uproar. Aboriginal/Torres Strait Islander people do not deserve any less.

When it comes to dismantling the systems which have been designed to oppress us, one statement rings clear. It came from the late Rosalie Kunoth-Monks in 2014, and was made more visible by Tarneen Onus-Williams's T-shirt at the Narrm Invasion Day rally in 2018: *I am not the problem*.

The media can bring us the stories, but they must be responded to. It is not enough to despair in front of the TV, to feel regret and guilt, to express alarm and upset, and then do nothing. It takes determination and energy to forge change. Aboriginal/Torres Strait Islander people are constantly using our energy, we are always alert and responding, and we are not solitary—we exist in relationships with each other as a community, a collective. We are strategic, intelligent, wise and hold knowledge. But we are also busy and tired. When news stories break like the ones described here, our busyness and fatigue mean we are not always ready or willing to talk through the issues. They are painful and can bring up trauma. We will comment on or talk about things on our own terms. We are not sitting by our computers waiting for a barrage of emails and social media comments from White people asking for answers from us. We are doing enough. It is non-Indigenous people who need to do more.

Individual responsibility must be built upon to create change in mainstream settings, and more broadly within White Australia. Yet collective responsibility wanes in the face of globalisation, with social media usage surging, a greater emphasis being placed on white-collar work, and politicians displaying 'Let them eat cake' attitudes towards their constituents. World events like the COVID-19 pandemic have also shifted our priorities, and when a legitimate fear of the virus is combined with government inaction on protecting public health (in particular, the Commonwealth not ordering enough vaccines or rapid antigen tests), there is no greater sign that we are on our own. Slogans like 'We're all in this together' reek of privilege and don't account for differing experiences among people in our own communities. There is so much to be learned from how Aboriginal community–controlled health services respond in crises, drawing from millennia of teachings about the importance of caring for one another and maintaining kinships, mutual responsibilities, and preserving a strong sense of community. This isn't to say that non-Indigenous health professionals are not doing amazing work—they are. But when governments fail to appreciate and invest in areas like health and community-building, individualists rise to perpetuate 'Me first, others last' as the norm.

Social media does make our stories more accessible and visible. For countless Aboriginal/Torres Strait Islander people, it is a way of sharing news, expressing our creativity, passing on knowledge, and storytelling. Major events can be engaged with freely, and starkly critiqued. In March 2022, the not guilty verdict in the trial of Zachary Rolfe, the police officer accused of killing Warlpiri man Kumanjayi Walker in the NT community of Yuendumu, solidified for Aboriginal/Torres Strait Islander people the understanding that our lives do not matter, and we took to social media to remind the world of this distressing fact. The Black Lives Matter movement began in mid-2013 with use of the hashtag #BlackLivesMatter on social media after George Zimmerman was acquitted in the shooting death of African American teenager Trayvon Martin. The call to action by the hashtag's originators—Alicia Garza, Patrisse Cullors and Opal Tometi—has since been taken up by communities across the globe, shining much-needed light on how White violence is systematically inflicted upon Black people, including here in Australia. Not only is this violence imposed, it is also often ignored, mostly excused, and frequently accepted as the natural order.

Both during and after the trial, Walker was portrayed by the prosecution and the mainstream media as a dangerous person, alongside disgraceful suggestions that he had brought his mortal fate upon himself. The verdict surfaced a cycle that @BundjalungBud expressed on Twitter as 'anger, sadness, fear, repeat'. When Rolfe went to trial, he was the first serving police officer in Australia to be charged with murder. Many people were convinced this was going to be the catalyst for change, that finally police would be held accountable, not only for using excessive force with Aboriginal/Torres Strait Islander people, but for killing them. What played out was a reinforcement of how the protection of the police force takes precedence over a young Aboriginal man's life.

Still, as trials like this play out in real time on social media, we can engage in ways we haven't been able to in the past. We can connect as an online community through platforms like Twitter to read live updates and understand the process, as well as grieve, rage and express our despair. The hashtag #BlackfullaTwitter supports this facet of our community. It is one way we can exercise our right to freedom of speech, and we exercise that right freely, loudly and unapologetically. White Australia sometimes interprets this as giving it free reign to say whatever it likes, but with rights come responsibilities, and freedom of speech is not a licence for hate speech. Turning up the decibels in protecting our rights is not a signal for racist, discriminatory commentary in response. In the words of the late Māori man Dr Moana Jackson, 'No one's exercise of free speech should make another feel less free.'

Since the Royal Commission into Aboriginal Deaths in Custody delivered its report in 1991, over 470 Aboriginal/Torres Strait Islander people have died in custody.[11] The royal commission made a total of 339 recommendations, and to this day not one of them has been implemented. There is no relief. We are in a constant state of grieving, torment and betrayal. When Rolfe's verdict was handed down, I felt devastated for the Walker family, and for our whole community. I thought, 'Why did we think it might be different this time?' Seeing senior Yuendumu Elders and members of the Walker family respond with deep reverence, stoicism and sorrow was gut-wrenching. We all felt their pain in that moment as they expressed their 'deep disappointment' with the outcome of the trial. But like any other story which tells of inhumanity and injustices brought against Aboriginal/Torres Strait Islander people, nothing will change if people just wring their hands while watching the news, then push it all to one side the next day—out of mind, out of sight.

The way in which our activism is organised and expressed continues to evolve, including how we engage with and use different forms of media. But some forms of activism have long sustained us. At the time of writing, it was the fiftieth anniversary of the establishment of the Aboriginal Tent Embassy on 26 January 1972. On that day, four Aboriginal men—Michael Anderson, Billy Craigie, Tony Coorey and Bertie Williams—travelled from Sydney to Canberra and set up a beach umbrella on the lawn in front of Parliament House (now Old Parliament House). They declared the site the Aboriginal Tent Embassy in response to the William McMahon government's refusal to acknowledge Aboriginal land rights, sovereignty or native title.

Gumbainggir man Professor Gary Foley wrote in his 2014 book on the subject that the term 'tent embassy' was purposely chosen, intended to serve as a reminder that Aboriginal people were living in substandard conditions and being treated 'like aliens in their own land'.[12]

The Aboriginal Tent Embassy grew from a beach umbrella into a collection of tents courtesy of Foley and other staunch activists of the time, such as Isabel Coe, John Newfong, Chicka Dixon and Gordon Briscoe, and over the decades it has been maintained by Aboriginal people committed to our sovereignty and our rights. I have visited the embassy many times while in Canberra, calling in to say hello and show support to whomever might be there on the day, as many other visitors do. It's a reminder that our fight continues, and that there are mob committed to maintaining that fight. It is a place that has united Aboriginal/Torres Strait Islander people in demanding our rights, and it is formally recognised as a site representing our political struggles. Over the years, it has experienced relocation around the grounds of Old Parliament House and other parts of Canberra, and been destroyed by storms and damaged by arson attacks. Yet it remains strong both in spirit and in its physical presence. After half a century, it is the longest continuous protest for land rights in the world.

The embassy has become an intergenerational movement for asserting our sovereignty. This is a collective responsibility shared across the country by all of our families and communities, a responsibility that persists while real change is denied—as has happened so many times in the past.

Gough Whitlam, who succeeded McMahon as prime minister, showed support for the embassy's aims when he said 'their case is beyond argument … because all of us as Australians are diminished while the Aborigines are denied their rightful place in this nation'.[13] In August 1975, Whitlam displayed his government's commitment to land rights by purchasing lands in the Northern Territory around Kalkarindji (formerly known as Wave Hill) from Vestey's meat-packing company on behalf of the Gurindji people. He returned the land through the gesture of pouring sand into Vincent Lingiari's hands, nine years after the Gurindji strike—also known as the Wave Hill walk-off—during which over 200 stockmen, domestic servants and their families protested poor working and living conditions. But the gesture would remain empty. Whitlam went on to draft the first Commonwealth legislation to grant land rights, but his government was dismissed before the legislation passed the Senate. The Gurindji people were left waiting once more.

Meanwhile, the Aboriginal Tent Embassy remains on the lawns of Old Parliament House, a guiding light for those of us standing strong in the face of storms, fire and wind.

~

Being born, and identifying as, Aboriginal/Torres Strait Islander in this country is political in nature, a message articulated by many people before me, including Professor Bronwyn Carlson, who has also written extensively on Aboriginal/Torres Strait Islander engagement with social media. In Professor Carlson's 2016 book *The Politics of Identity*, she explores how people come to know they are Aboriginal/Torres Strait Islander; what it means to them; how their identity is expressed; and how it makes them feel, including being recognised and/or called on to defend one's Indigenous status. The Commonwealth has attempted to distil this profoundly significant matter into a three-part, legal definition of Aboriginal/Torres Strait Islander people which comprises the elements of descent, self-identification and community acceptance. But many complexities apply to these three elements because of colonisation and can result in heavy burdens placed upon individuals who might be requested to prove their identity.

Having Indigenous heritage and being Aboriginal/Torres Strait Islander are two different things, a fact well understood by Blackfullas across the land. This was clearly articulated by Gamilaraay woman and lawyer Nat Cromb in 2021 while referring to a senator claiming Indigenous heritage and citing themselves as an authority when they declared the slogan 'Always Was Always Will Be' was offensive to Aboriginal people. Besides commenting that the senator obviously knew nothing of the origins of the slogan, Cromb explained that much more is involved than just heritage when it comes to identifying—heritage alone does not mean that you *are*. Being Aboriginal/Torres Strait Islander comes from connection to country and community, lived experience, cultural knowledge, and finding and knowing kinship/relational responsibilities. This is the work that needs to be done before speaking with authority—these are our responsibilities as Blackfullas.

Professor Marcia Langton has written that Aboriginal/Torres Strait Islander identity took shape in Australia around 1770–78. Before this time, our heritage and identity was always known. Professor Langton has also spoken of the way in which Aboriginality has been manufactured post-1788, and how a fabricated reality has developed in which those who claim an Indigenous identity are then expected to perform it. The assertion and negotiation of our identities in a colonial environment evolves depending on personal experience and other factors such as community protocols and non-Indigenous pressures or expectations. I have always known I am Aboriginal, as I have always known that I have Irish and German heritage. These are all important parts of my identity. I am a product of how Australia was founded. But Professor Ian Anderson has written that our colonial history has rendered many Aboriginal/Torres Strait Islander people 'neither one nor the other', and that our identities are formed within the context of colonial relations.[14] Furthermore, Dad has often reminded me (and others through his publications) that we must resist being fixed into one way of being. Colonial essentialism around our identities categorises us into foreign ideals of what it is to be Aboriginal/Torres Strait Islander, but we have the right and freedom to transform and vary who we are and how we identify. We should not be secured within our identities by a colonial, racist measure of our blood. We exist and belong in relationships with our history, environments, ways of living, communities, and other elements of our cultures.

It is vital that we acknowledge and respect the fact that Aboriginal/Torres Strait Islander people are diverse in our identities, regardless of appearance or complexion. We comprise over 250 language groups, including around 800 dialects, each sacred and unique to a particular place and people.[15] Since the British invasion and the removal, denial and genocide of our languages, connections and bodies, the exemplification of our identities and learning about who we are have been occurring simultaneously across generations. An Elder who was stolen from their parents may be just beginning to discover family while having remained strong with their identity, at the same time as their children or grandchildren are just beginning to grow into their identities.

Young Aboriginal/Torres Strait Islander people learn from their own families and communities about ways to identify and express their own identity, which includes wearing the colours of our flags or other cultural adornments/clothing—something that newly discovered Aboriginal/Torres Strait Islander people often do, too. The Aboriginal fashion houses Gammin Threads and Haus of Dizzy provide helpful indicators to customers on their websites as to which items are 'mob only' or 'ally friendly'. These indicators help Aboriginal/Torres Strait Islander people keep visual parts of our identities just for us, purposely withholding them from allies (or others) who may appropriate them to perpetuate a false representation that they, too, are Aboriginal/Torres Strait Islander people.

Appropriating our identities is akin to appropriating our experiences, which is an assault on who we are and shows enormous contempt and disrespect. Allowing people to believe you are Aboriginal/

Torres Strait Islander when you are not, and not correcting people who assume you are, is revolting. We, as sovereign Aboriginal/Torres Strait Islander people, are the ones who decide who has kinship, who is part of our community, and who we claim. I have seen non-Indigenous people appropriate our identities and misrepresent themselves too many times, resulting in damage to the Aboriginal/Torres Strait Islander community. It exposes the lengths some non-Indigenous people are willing to go to. They particularly sicken me when they dare to speak in language in a room where they know Aboriginal/Torres Strait Islanders sit, performing our sacred cultures to us who have not had the chance to learn and grow in our own languages. The very caucasity of it enrages me. Once again, we are not the problem here.

~

I was fortunate in 1993 to accompany Dad to Geneva for a meeting of the Working Group on Indigenous Populations (later replaced by the Expert Mechanism on the Rights of Indigenous Peoples), of which he was a member. It was my first international flight, and due to Dad and I departing from different cities, I was an 'unaccompanied minor' with a string of enthusiastic flight attendants to help me during the long haul from Melbourne to Bangkok and Zurich, and finally to Geneva. The working group was beginning to draft what would become the United Nations Declaration on the Rights of Indigenous Peoples (UNDRIP), and it was an eye-opening and culturally nurturing experience for me, being surrounded by Indigenous peoples from across the world who were so like me yet so different. The global connection I've felt in international conference rooms since shows me that there is an undeniable spirit and link that Indigenous peoples have despite geographic or political boundaries.

Observing Dad and his international colleagues collectively contribute to UNDRIP, an instrument of social justice and change, also helped me learn how I, too, have responsibilities as a change-maker—it reinforced what Dad had already told us kids, that we were experts in our rights due to their absence. This was one of the many significant events that shaped my identity in the early 1990s. And I will never forget driving through the streets of Geneva one balmy evening in our hire car, windows down, with 'Treaty' blaring through the stereo. When I said that song was everywhere at the time, you can bet it was because of Blackfullas with cassette tapes in hand.

Seventeen years later, in 2010, I once again accompanied Dad to the UN, this time in New York, not only as his daughter but as his assistant at the Permanent Forum on Indigenous Issues. Dad was the expert member for Australia at the forum, in his final year in the role (he was succeeded by Cobble Cobble woman Professor Megan Davis), and it was a huge opportunity to see how the UN worked with Dad still connected in this way. So I took annual leave from my job and paid my way to the Big Apple to sit by his side in the General Assembly. What a privilege, and again, what an eye-opening and culturally nurturing experience. At the time I was yearning to go back to study, and this trip solidified for me that I wanted to do a master's in human rights law. Not to practise law, mind you—I have friends and family members who are lawyers, including some deadly Black lawyers! That is not my calling. Rather, my endeavour was to apply my degree to increasing access to, and ensuring social justice in, education for Aboriginal/Torres Strait Islander people, particularly higher education. I would complete my degree through the Castan Centre for Human Rights Law while working at Monash University, and I am forever grateful to the colleagues there who supported me, including Professor Adam Shoemaker and Dr Melissa Castan—examples of allies who truly understand how supporting Aboriginal/Torres Strait Islander people in the right ways leads to great outcomes.

Our rights are enshrined in UNDRIP, with the right to identify as Aboriginal/Torres Strait Islander people including being free from any kind of discrimination. When the UN finally voted to adopt the declaration in 2007, there were four dissenters: the United States of America, Canada, New Zealand and Australia. See a pattern there? All are settler colonies of the British Empire with majority non-Indigenous populations. (All four countries have since moved to endorse the declaration, but in ways that ensure it does not become applicable or binding by law—this occurred in Australia in 2009 via Kevin Rudd's government.) The reasons for Australia's dissent, voiced by the John Howard government, included concerns about references to our self-determination being mis-construed, the extension of Indigenous intellectual property rights, and the placement of Indigenous customary law in a superior position to national law—for example, in the case of customary corporal and capital punishment. The Howard government could not be described as having been committed to the protection of Indigenous rights. A decade earlier, it had concerned itself with amending the *Native Title Act* after the High Court delivered the Wik judgment, wielding a 'Ten Point Plan' designed to respond to mining companies and pastoralists who wanted native title extinguished so they could continue to operate. I will never forget the feeling in the room at the Melbourne Convention Centre in 1996 when Howard yelled and banged his fist on the lectern, angrily trying to convince us, as we all turned our backs to him in a unifying display of resistance to his commitment to the colonial project on our lands.

Howard also showed his apathy and inaction regarding the protection of Indigenous rights when the Commonwealth suspended the *Racial Discrimination Act* in 2007 to impose the Northern Territory Emergency Response (NTER, also known as the Intervention). Before continuing, I should acknowledge that I have never lived in the Northern Territory, and these are not my communities (notwithstanding my Granny Liz being a Gurindji woman). The wants and needs of those communities are theirs to articulate and demand, not mine. However, I nonetheless would like to point out that, in 2009, Professor James Anaya, the then UN special rapporteur on Indigenous rights, was invited to visit Aboriginal communities in the Northern Territory. His key findings were that no consultations had taken place with these communities prior to NTER, and that key aspects of the Intervention limited the capacity of Indigenous individuals and communities to control or participate in decisions affecting their own lives, property and cultural development.[16] Professor Anaya stated that the Intervention discriminated based on race, thereby raising serious human rights concerns. Howard's response to Professor Anaya's findings was disinterest, brushing them off as merely one man's opinion, and arguing that the UN had no right to interfere in Australian domestic affairs.[17] How were we supposed to have our rights protected with attitudes like that?

Australia does not have a bill of rights, but Victoria does have a Charter of Human Rights and Responsibilities, which came into force in 2006. The Victorian Equal Opportunity and Human Rights Commission is responsible for the assessment of, and education of the public on, the charter, which enshrines civil, political and cultural rights into Victorian law, ensuring rights such as freedom of speech have legal protection. The charter is important because, in the absence of a national bill of rights, it sets a standard for the Victorian community, one that says all people have value and should be able to live lives free of discrimination. It provides a way for truths about how some people are treated in our society to be aired and resolved, so that injustices can be prevented from reoccurring. Sadly, as many of my stories and recollections illustrate, Aboriginal/Torres Strait Islander people know and experience injustices too frequently.

Yoorrook is the Wemba Wemba word for truth. The Wemba Wemba people belong to areas in northern Victoria and southern New South Wales, on either side of the Murray River, covering places now known as Swan Hill, Kerang, Deniliquin, Quambatook and Lake Boga. The Yoorrook Justice

Commission was established in Victoria in 2022 to serve as an official inquiry into the impact of colonisation on First Nation peoples in Victoria. It is the first of its kind in Australia and has powers much like a royal commission. The origins of the Yoorrook Justice Commission lie in consultations between the First Peoples' Assembly and Aboriginal communities in Victoria in 2020, when it was made clear the treaty process could not advance without an opportunity for truth-telling.[18] This step in uncovering truths, through an Aboriginal-led commission, will undoubtedly influence the treaty process in a solid and positive way, and hopefully bring some healing and reparations to those who have been wronged.

~

In Yawuru, we say *liyarn*, which means spirit. This is the basis of our resilience. It is the core of our existence, derived from our kinships and ways of knowing, doing and being. *Mabu liyarn* means good spirit, and that is what we have when we are connected to family, country and community. But we can't have collective *mabu liyarn* when our rights are being violated, and this is the reason my family does the work that we do. In my work, I use the rights we have as Indigenous people to guide strategies and decision-making, and to influence others around me. Rights-based approaches bring better social justice outcomes where things like RAPs can't. A RAP can give us hope for change, but truth-telling and justice require greater strategy and commitment.

I used to think that hope was a form of resistance. Maybe it still is, at times? Having hope, I think, is a sign of optimism, and it can belong both to the privileged and the deprived. My views on hope shifted when I read Munanjahli/South Sea Islander woman Professor Chelsea Watego's 2021 book *Another Day in the Colony*, which was written clearly and unapologetically for the mob. Professor Watego is unwavering in her message to us that we should not be hopeful but sovereign, for it is through our sovereignty that we remind the colonisers that we are still here, that they didn't succeed. Never have, never will.[19]

We who are Aboriginal/Torres Strait Islander people have never ceded our sovereignty, and we identify ourselves as individuals, families and communities in the way we see fit. There are both solo and shared expressions of who we are, and we shall not be forced to pick or choose any one way to be according to others' instructions or expectations. Similarly, we shall not be forced to pick or choose which rights and how much social justice we are afforded. It is not 'one or the other' when it comes to treaty and land rights, truth-telling and recognition. We deserve all of our rights, and that means not having to compromise.

Rubibi/Broome, Pyipkil/Port Fairy and Narrm/ Melbourne are places I am connected to, places that continue to generously provide me with *mabu liyarn*. They give me everything I need to be strong and grounded in my identity, with connections to who I am as a Yawuru woman, and connections to the communities I live and work in. Goorie woman and author Melissa Lucashenko has said, 'Write what your truth is,'[20] and that is what I have done here. My experience as an Aboriginal person is unique to me, but it may also ring true to other Blackfullas. What I'm doing is for my nieces and nephews, and my son, in the names of our ancestors and Elders. Our young people are smart, strategic, resolute, and strong in culture. They are leaders who continue to learn across the generations and push for change.

There is still much work to be done. It calls me constantly, so I cannot rest. I am obliged to persevere to ensure the *marrul*—the changing wind—keeps blowing strongly.

ACKNOWLEDGEMENTS

I never thought I could or would write a book, but here it is! I could not have done this without the belief of people around me, especially my husband Ishan and son Buddy. Thank you, my guys. Thanks also to the rest of my family, who continue to support me, teach me and keep me accountable. I also thank Louise Adler, Paul Smitz and Lisa Millar, who helped make this possible.

My community holds great knowledge and excellence, and I want to acknowledge the leadership and support of the following people who continue to guide me: Aunty Anne Martin, Professor Aunty Bronwyn Fredericks, Dr Leanne Holt, Professor Aunty Marcia Langton, Professor Shaun Ewen, Professor Uncle Peter Yu, Tiriki Onus, Aunty Carolyn Briggs, Uncle Paul Briggs, Aunty June Oscar, Aunty Pam Pederson, Aunty Di Kerr and many others—thank you.

NOTES

1   Kevin Keeffe, *Paddy's Road: Life Stories of Patrick Dodson*, Aboriginal Studies Press, Canberra, 2003.

2   See Family Matters, '*Family Matters Report 2020* Reveals Aboriginal and Torres Strait Islander Children Continue to Be Separated from Families and Culture at an Alarming Rate', 16 November 2020, https://www.familymatters.org.au/family-matters-report-2020-reveals-aboriginal-and-torres-strait-islander-children-continue-to-be-separated-from-families-and-culture-at-an-alarming-rate (viewed April 2022).

3   As told by the family; also cited in Keeffe, *Paddy's Road*.

4   Christopher Warren, 'Smallpox at Sydney Cove: Who, When, Why?', *Journal of Australian Studies*, vol. 38, no. 1, 2014, pp. 68–86.

5   Keeffe, *Paddy's Road*.

6   Uncle Pat Dodson, from 'Patrick Dodson: Father of Reconciliation', *Living Black*, series 27, episode 7, NITV/SBS, 25 May 2020.

7   Derived from *kareela*, most probably a Dharawal/Gweagal/Eora word.

8   Max Gillies, from *Hawke: The Larrikin and the Leader*, ABC TV, February 2018.

9   Paul Keating, 'Transcript: Redfern Speech', 10 December 1992, Australians for Native Title and Reconciliation, https://antar.org.au/sites/default/files/paul_keating_speech_transcript.pdf (viewed April 2022).

10   Gregory Phillips, 'Can We Breathe?', IndigenousX, 31 December 2020, https://indigenousx.com.au/can-we-breathe (viewed April 2022).

11   T Anthony, K Jordan, T Walsh, F Markham and M Williams, *30 Years on: Royal Commission into Aboriginal Deaths in Custody Recommendations Remain Unimplemented*, Centre for Aboriginal Economic Policy Research, ANU College of Arts & Social Sciences, no. 140, 2021.

12   Gary Foley and Andrew Schaap (eds), *The Aboriginal Tent Embassy: Sovereignty, Black Power, Land Rights and the State*, Routledge, Abingdon, UK, 2013.

13   Gough Whitlam, from *Sovereignty: 50 Years of the Tent Embassy*, ABC TV, 29 January 2022.

14   Bronwyn Carlson, *The Politics of Identity: Who Counts as Aboriginal Today?*, Aboriginal Studies Press, Canberra, 2016.

15   Australian Institute of Aboriginal and Torres Strait Islander Studies, 'Living Languages', AIATSIS, 2022, https://aiatsis.gov.au/explore/living-languages (viewed April 2022).

16   James Anaya, *Observations on the Northern Territory Emergency Response in Australia*, United Nations, Geneva, 1 February 2010.

17   L Royer, 'Using One's Right of Inspection: Australia, the United Nations, Human Rights and Aboriginal People', *Revue LISA*, 4 December 2014.

18   Yoorrook Justice Commission, 'Overview', 2021, https://yoorrookjusticecommission.org.au/overview (viewed April 2022).

19   Chelsea Watego, *Another Day in the Colony*, University of Queensland Press, Indooroopilly, Qld, 2021.

20   Sarah Malik, 'Melissa Lucashenko, Write What Your Truth Is', SBS, 4 August 2020, https://www.sbs.com.au/topics/voices/culture/article/2020/06/19/melissa-lucashenko-writing-era-black-lives-matter (viewed April 2022).